The Show Must Go On

A Comical Farcical Musical

Book, Music and Lyrics

By Mike Daniel

Absidy Publishing Company ™
Anaheim, CA

For more information about the works of
Michael Daniel, visit http://michaeldaniel.net

Cast of Characters:

Cure—Friend of Stu. Works to get Stu and Elemenope together.

Elemenope—Daughter of Sediefge. Excessively happy in all situations.

Sediefge (See-dee-ef-geh)—Father of Elemenope. Town nobleman. Very protective of only child, Elemenope, unless tempted by "worldly objects with optical attraction."

Xyze (Zi-zee)—Wife of Sediefge.

Stu—A peasant. In love with Elemenope.

Abie (Ay-bee)—A peasant girl. In love with Stu.

High Jack (a.k.a Sir Bruswayne [Bru-swain])—A pirate who kidnaps Elemenope and Abie.

View—High Jack's first mate.

Tuthrie (Tooth-ree)—A retired pirate.

The Statue[1]—A statue of the town's founder, William Nineten. The statue reacts to the action in the play, but is never seen moving by the characters until the last scene.

The Mysterious Off-Stage Voice—'Nuff said.

The Peasants/Pirates/Three Dancer Girls/A Drunken Priest/Thee Policemen

---

[1] A Note on the Statue: Stage directions for the Statue are intentionally vague, for there are a few ways that this character can be played. The author's original vision was an actor who would stand completely still throughout the play up until the moment when he speaks to Stu. However, in the original OPF production, the Statue reacted to what was going on on-stage and acted as a sort of "Greek solo." Either technique is equally effective and funny.

Musical Numbers
Act I

"The Show Must Go On"..............................Cure
"Smile"..Elemenope
"Watching Her".................................Stu, Abie
"There is a Way"....................................Cure
"Worldly Objects With Optical Attraction".....Sediefge
"There's Only One Fish in the Sea for Me"..........Stu,
Cure, Abie, View
"I'll go to the End of the World For Her".............Stu
"That is How You Win the Girls"....................Men
"Dance For Us".....................................Pirates
"Smile (Reprise)".......................Elemenope, Abie
"The Show Must Go On (Act I Finale)"........Company

Act II

"There He Is"..Abie
"Happy Day!"...................................Company
"Worldly Objects With Optical Attraction (Reprise)"...
Sediefge, Xyze
"I'll go to the End of the World For Him"...........Abie
"Wedding Plans"...................Elemenope, Sediefge,
Xyze, Abie, Cure
"There's a Wedding Today".....................Company
"I Want a Damn Song!".................High Jack, View,
Priest, Peasants
"Worldly Objects With Optical Attraction (Reprise)"...
Sediefge
"How Can I Go On?"...................................Stu
"Keep Your Head Up High"..........................Statue
"I'll be There For You"...........................Abie, Stu
"The Show Must Go On (Finale)"...............Company

THE SHOW MUST GO ON premiered on Monday, August 13th 2001 at the Aloha Theater as the opening performance for the Kona Association for the Performing Arts' Seventh Annual Original Play Festival (OPF). It was directed by BRUCE MONACO. BERNALDO EVANGELISTA provided accompaniment on the keyboard. Choral directors were ARLENE ARAKI and ARDETH WEED. The dances were choreographed by NANI MOREMAN. The cast was as follows:

Cure...Felix Cabrera

Elemenope...........................Leah Simon-Westreich

Sediefge.......................................L. Bernard Marsh

Xyze..Rebecca Marsh

Stu...Mike Daniel

Abie.............................Shanna Simon-Westreich

High Jack.....................................Blake McMillen

View...Roxanne Fox

Tuthrie......................................Dick Hershberger

The Statue....................................Robin Hurlbut

The Mysterious Off-Stage Voice..........Robert Curtis

A Drunken Priest...............................Rob Rhine

Chorus........Arlene Araki, Jessie Cardin, Amy Jaeger, Gregory Mason, Analie Montany, Nani Moreman, Anna Northrop, Shannon Northrop, Terrence O'Brien, Toriana Rohan, Kevin Ruel, Ardeth Weed

Dancer Girls...........Analia Montany, Nani Moreman, Shannon Northrop, Amy Jaeger

For Liz,
I know you don't particularly want this, but I wrote it for you
and it didn't seem right dedicating it to anyone else.

Act I

Setting: *(The town center. At C. stands the STATUE, standing on a pedestal and wearing a 'coonskin' cap. On top of the STATUE'S hat stands a statue of a cat, on top of which is a statue of a bird, on top of which is a statue of a mouse. At C. stands the house of SEDIEFGE. The house is a two-story structure. The top story is nothing more than a balcony with an off-stage ladder leading up to it. On the bottom story is a doorstep and a door. As the AUDIENCE enters, the CREW is on stage making repairs to the set. A tall ladder stands U.L. where a CREWMAN is making repairs. Until the* Overture *begins, various super-stitious omens occur: a black cat runs across the stage; a mirror breaks back-stage; one of the CREWMEN spills salt on the stage; another CREWMAN is constantly talking about how the set for MACBETH will be much easier to deal with; etc. When it is time to begin, the CREWMEN casually exit. The ladder U.L. is left on-stage. The CONDUCTOR enters and begins the* Overture. *Suddenly, the ACTOR playing CURE runs on stage in a robe and bunny slippers from U.L. As he runs on, he runs underneath the ladder. He tries to get the attention of the CONDUCTOR, who is in the middle of conducting the* Overture.*)*

Cure: *(Losing his patience.)* Cut the music!!!

(The CONDUCTOR, infuriated, hurls his baton at CURE who deftly ducks away from it.)

Cure: *(Sarcastically to CONDUCTOR.)* Thank you. *(To AUDIENCE.)* Good evening. I regret to inform you

1

that there has been a rather unpleasant accident back stage—the actor playing the character of Stu, David Hasselhoff *(or ad-lib some other* "specially talented" *actor; Keanu Reeves, Tobey Maguire, Christopher Walken, you get the idea.)*, has just slipped on a bowl of dog food and shall not be able to perform for you tonight. But, you are in luck, for the understudy, *(Says the REAL ACTOR'S name)*, is close at hand and shall be available to perform this evening! After all, the show must go on!

> *(Sings.)*
> Here in the theater
> An'thing can go wrong.
> It doesn't matter
> The show must go on!
>
> Stabbings or muggings,
> Jabbings or thuggings,
> Still doesn't matter,
> The show must go on!
>
> Sandbags may fall,
> Set parts may break,
> Cupid may call
> During an earthquake.

(spoken, music under) Allow myself to introduce myself and welcome you to our small town of Absidy. My name is Cure and I am but a simple peasant of this quaint town. *(Indicating the STATUE.)* This wonderful work of art which you see here is the statue of our humble town's not-so-humble founder, William Nineten. No one knows the exact significance of the animals on his head. Perhaps it was to represent the fierce household pets and rodents that inhabited the meadow in which the foundation of this town is built.

(The STATUE, unnoticed by CURE, waves at the audience.)

Cure: *(sings)*
> Singers may miss notes
> Actors make misquotes
> Even for a moron,
> The show must bore on!

(spoken - indicating the house of SEDIEFGE, music under)
This is the house of Sediefge, the town nobleman. And that lovely young woman there - *(indicating ELEME-NOPE, who has just walked out onto the balcony and is looking out on the town, smiling profusely)* - is his beautiful daughter Elemenope. To all you young men out there in the audience, you had best not waste your time there for her father will only marry her to a man of high rank. *(Confidentially.)* Or to the man who has the prettiest jewels.

Elemenope: *(sings)*
> Machines may break down,
> Still it must go on.
> Whatever goes wrong,
> Don't show a frown!

Cure: *(as STU enters, music under)* Ah! Our hero arrives! This strapping young lad is of course none other than my dearest, sweetest, most beloved, and humbly humble friend, Stu. *(STU, unaware of CURE, only dotes upon ELEMENOPE.)* Stu, as you perhaps can tell, is somewhat smitten with the aforementioned woman whose only chance of marriage will be through an arrangement of family jewels. Alas, poor Stu, a

3

peasant like yours truly, stands no chance of winning the fair lass's hand.

(STU sighs extremely over-dramatically.)

Cure: *(music under)* And now, it is with my most sincerely and profoundly immense and satisfactory pleasure that I am honored with the most gratifyingly complimentary role of introducing you to our exquisitely costumed and pleasantly in-tune Company!

COMPANY: *(entering, sings)*
>Sandbags may fall,
>Set parts may break,
>Cupid may call
>During an earthquake!
>
>Actors may miss cues
>Taking a quick snooze
>Whatever goes wrong,
>The show must go on!
>
>Stabbings or muggings,
>Jabbings or thuggings,
>Still doesn't matter,
>The show must go on!

Cure: *(sings)*
>The show must go on!

Cure: *(spoken, music under.)*[2]
After all, the odds of any of these things actually happening are about nilch! *(Orchestra finishes the song.)*[3] And now, with out any further delay, the show must go on.

(The PEASANTS begin miming various conversations and shopping for various things as CURE exits and ELEMENOPE, up on her balcony, takes the stage.)

Elemenope: *(Sings.)*
>   My father always told me to smile,
>   No matter what.
>   Whatever happens don't lose your guile,
>   It's what you've got.

>   For a smile can go a long, long way.
>   A smile can change another person's day.
(Her smile growing until it's almost painfully wide.)
>   So I smile, and I smile, and I smile, and I smile
>   All the whole long while.

>   I don't know much about
>   Anything.
>   I don't know arithmetic
>   Or how to add.

>   Who cares if I can't hold a conversation?
>   Smart people are so dull and boring.

---

[2] If the audience starts to applaud before the following line, cut them off and ad-lib a line something like "No, not yet. The song's not over yet. Geez." If they don't applaud, just continue.
[3] If the audience, trained by the previous scenario, does not applaud at the end of the song, ad-lib a line somethinglike "Ok, you can applaud now."

I don't know about stuff like conservatation,
But I know that stuff makes me start snoring.

And I know a smile is like a candy cane,
A smile can take away the need for a brain.
(Smile growing.)
So I smile, and I smile, and I smile, and I smile,
Although it may seem juvenile.
(Hums merrily.)

(The PEASANT MEN have gathered below her balcony, gaping at her beauty. SEDIEFGE and XYZE exit the house, arm in arm. SEDIEFGE chases the MEN away, shouting at them. Music ends.)

Sediefge: *(Chasing the MEN away.)* Scram! Get out of here! I'll not have you vagrants ogling at my daughter!

Xyze: *(Trying to calm him down.)* Come, come, Sediefge. You can't hide Elemenope from the world forever. She's a blossoming young woman.

Sediefege: I'll be damned before I marry my only child off to anyone without noble rank, Xyze. It would be a disgrace to our family name!

Xyze: *(Leading him off U.L.)* Dear, you really do have to try not to be so overprotective...

Sediefge: *(muttering under his breath as they leave)* I'll be over-protective of you...

(As they leave, lights come up on STU who is sitting on the pedestal, watching ELEMENOPE, who is standing on her balcony, doing nothing but looking pretty. ABIE

approaches him and sits down next to him on the pedestal.)

Abie: *(flirtatiously, music under.)* So, Stu, what's on your mind?

Stu: *(absent-mindedly, music under.)* Oh, hi Abie. Nothing much. Just her.

Abie: *(somewhat disappointed.)* Who?

Stu: Elemenope.
    (Sings.)
    Watching her
    Is like watching the sunrise
    Each day.
    Watching her
    Is like smelling a row of pies,
    I say.

    I watch her with my eyes,
    And my sun begins to rise.
    My heart begins to race,
    And yet, I can't say so to her face.

    Watching her,
    My heart begins to race
    Right now.
    Watching her,
    I know my place
    In life.

    I feel her with my soul,
    And ev'rything feels right.
    I'll go where she will go.

For her life, a pirate I will fight!
(spoken, music under)
You can honestly have no idea of the depth of my feelings, Abie.

Abie: *(sings)*
>   Watching you
>   Is like watching the sunrise,
>   I swear.
>   Watching you,
>   I feel my soul rise.

(Sighing, as she realizes he's not even paying attention.)
>   You don't care.

>   I know you in my heart,
>   I'll go where you will go.
>   I can't stand to be apart,
>   And yet, you do not know

Together: *(sing)*
>   I'm watching you/her.

(ABIE, hurt, runs off, holding back tears. STU, of course, is too entranced with ELEMENOPE to even notice. CURE, waking up, crawls out from behind the statue and sits down next to STU. He is carrying a satchel with him.)

Cure: *(Yawning.)* My, it is a wonderful day, isn't it?

Stu: *(Sighing.)* Yes, it is.

Cure: What are you so dreamy about?

Stu: Cure, I have fallen in love with the fairest maiden in all the land. A maiden who could make any man's heart feel like that of a prince.

Cure: Ah, Elizabeth. Yes, she is quite a catch, if I may say so myself.

Stu: No.

Cure: Come, come, my dear man. You can't go on pretending that you're the only man alive who finds her attractive.

Stu: No, I mean it's not Elizabeth.

Cure: Oh. Well, it must be Rebecca then, am I right?

Stu: No.

Cure: Susanna?

Stu: No.

Cure: Ariel?

Stu: No.

Cure: Well, it must be Jul—

Stu: *(Losing his patience.)* Cure, it's Elemenope who has won my heart.

Cure: *(A slight, awkward pause.)* Elemenope? Yes, of course. Elemenope. She was my next guess. *(Aside.)* Well, this is quite a dilemma. Surely I can't tell him about my secret engagement to Elemenope. The poor guy would be crushed. There must be some way to distract him. *(Getting an idea.)* Of course! *(He pulls out of his satchel a rather large book and begins leafing through it.)* I'll just consult my handy "Cupid's Official Guide to Love Encyclopedia." *(To the audience.)* Sorry, it was a limited edition and all the other copies went up in the big fire and I'm sure not about to give it up. *(Pats it light-heartedly, then continues browsing.)* Let's see…ah, here we are.

The Mysterious Off-Stage Voice: *(Reciting as CURE reads.)* Your lower-class best friend has fallen in love with your upper-class secret fiance and you don't have the guts to tell him the truth, you cowardly little snip.

Cure: *(To the audience.)* Wow, this book has *everything*!

TMOSV: *(Continuing.)* Try setting them up.

Cure: *(Confused.)* Huh?

TMOSV: No, really. The fact of the matter is that the odds of an upper class girl falling for a low-life commoner are about nilch.

Cure: *(Offended.)* Hey, *I'm* a low-life commoner! I mean—

TMOSV: The fact that she has fallen for you is a pure coincidence and coincidences almost never happen twice, therefore the odds of her falling for him are next to nothing. When your match-making fails, he will go on his way, broken hearted, and you can have your girl.

Or, of course, you could always arrange to have her kidnapped by pirates.

Cure: *(Closing the book.)* I think I'll go with plan A.

Stu: *(Sighing, still in a trance.)* There must be a way.

Cure: *(Getting an idea, sings.)*
    Of course, it's true,
    There is a way!
    It's like you said,
    There must be a way!

    You said she makes
    You feel like a prince
    It can't be too hard
    To make you into a prince.

Stu: *(Music Under)* A prince? No way.

Cure: *(Sings.)*
    Now hear me out,
    And see what it's about.
    It's really quite simple,
    Easier than squeezing a pimple.

(STU makes a disgusted face.)

Cure: *(Sings.)*
    We'll clean you up,
    Make you look all nice.
    We'll have to wash your hair,
    (Picking something out of STU'S hair.)
    Get rid of the lice.

11

But once we get
You looking all nice,
Any girl would pay a price
To make you an om'let!

We'll get you a robe,
A whole new wardrobe!
We'll make you look so good and nice,
Old Seedy won't think twice!

Stu: *(Music under.)* But what if he should recognize me?

Cure: *(Sings.)*
We'll get you some glasses,
They're easy to rent.
You'll easily pass as—
(STU looks at CURE quizzically.)
Hey, it worked for Clark Kent!
(Spoken, music under.)
In fact, that's what we'll call you: Prince Clarkent!

Stu: *(Music under.)* What if Sediefge won't marry Elemenope off to a prince he's never heard of?

Cure: *(Sings.)*
Silly boy, it's not the name,
It's not even the fame.
No, old Seedy makes the rules
By the prettiness of the jewels.

Stu: *(Music under.)* And how will we pay for the jewels and the royal robes.

Cure: *(Sings.)*
>Why I'll—*(Catching himself.)*
>Oh, wait I'm poor.
>Oh what a bore.
>*(Pacing.)*
>There must be a way,
>There must be a way...

(The scene between CURE and STU freezes as HIGH JACK and VIEW enter, disguised as noblemen.)

High Jack: *(Sighing, music under.)* You know something, View?

View: *(Music under.)* What, High Jack?

High Jack: *(Lashing out.)* Don't call me High Jack here. The town's people cannot know my secret identity. You must call me by my alias, Sir Bruswayne, whenever we are incognito.

View: Right High Jack. Sorry High Jack. Forgive me High Jack. As you were saying High Jack.

High Jack: View, I've grown tired of my current collection of female entertainers. You can only play the same tune so many times before it gets old. It's time that we add some spice to my collection of concubines.

View: I'm sorry, sir, but I don't believe in cannibalism. It goes against my Pirate's Code of Ethics.

High Jack: View, I don't mean literally add spice. I mean we need some fresh flesh. New territory to plunder, if you will.

13

View: Oh, of course! Right, right! I gotcha, High Jack.

High Jack: I'm sure that there must be some fair damsels in this town who are looking to be put into distress.

View: *(confused)* But High Jack, you're not wearing a dress.

High Jack: *(irritated)* Not "this dress," *"distress,"* you provincial putz! *(VIEW doesn't understand.)* D-I-S-T-R-E-S-S! *Distress!*

View: Oh, right High Jack!

High Jack: *(muttering to himself)* What am I ever going to do with him? *(He looks up and sees ELEMENOPE on her balcony, smiling at the world.)* Well, hello miss!

(The scene between CURE and STU unfreezes and HIGH JACK overhears their conversation.)

Cure: *(Sings.)*
>There must be a way!
>There must be a way!
>There must be a way
>To get you and Elemenope together!

High Jack: *(Cutting in, end of music.)* Excuse me, kind sirs, I could not help but overhear your conversation. Could it be that the woman you refer to is that young girl standing on the balcony?

Cure: This is so, but you had best not waste your time, sir. For her father is a tyrant who will only marry her off to a suitor of noble status.

High Jack: Well, you are in luck, my good men. I am Sir Bruswayne. I come here from a far-off land and I shall be leaving in the morning. I would be more than willing to pose as a suitor for that young woman to get her away from the house so that she and your young friend here—

Stu: *(Interrupting.)* Stu.

High Jack: —Stu. So that the young lady and Stu can elope.

Stu: *(Ecstatic.)* Oh, kind sir, I would be most grateful!

High Jack: Do not mention it. Now, if I may inquire, where are the girl's parents at this moment.

Stu: *(Pointing off U.L.)* Why, here they come now.

(XYZE and SEDIEFGE enter with bags of groceries, still bickering.)

Sediefge: For the last and final time, Xyze, I shall not have my only daughter married to a commoner! I simply will not allow it.

(HIGH JACK approaches them and offers his hand. Out of habit, they offer theirs too, dropping their groceries to the ground.)

High Jack: *(As he helps them gather their groceries.)* Oh, goodness me! Look what I've done. Truly sorry. *(As they rise.)* Sorry about that. Allow me to introduce myself, I am Sir Bruswayne. I have traveled across land and sea to ask you for the hand of your daughter—

Stu: *(Whispering her name to him.)* Elemenope!

High Jack: —Elemenope.

Xyze: *(Ecstatic.)* Oh, happy day! What wonderful news! Elemenope will be so delighted!

Sediefge: *(Suspiciously.)* Strange, I have never heard of anyone by the name of "Sir Bruswayne."

(HIGH JACK reaches into his purse, pulls out a ruby necklace and casually begins admiring it. SEDIEFGE is entranced.)

Sediefge: *(Sings.)*
>Rubies!
>Oh, how I love my rubies!
>Oh, how I love my worldly objects
>With optical attraction!
>
>See how they shine!
>Ooh, if only they all were mine!
>Oh, how I love my rubies!
>Oh, how I love my jewels.

(spoken, regaining his composure.) Oh, what delightful news! Come, come inside with us! We must introduce you to Elemenope at once!

(As they disappear into the house, STU begins jumping up and down, celebrating his pending success. CURE, as always, remains calm and neutral. ABIE re-enters, having regained her composure, and overhears the conversation.)

Stu: We did it, Cure! By William Nineten we did it!

Cure: Now Stu, don't go counting your omelets before they cook.

View: *(Approaching them.)* What's the big deal, boy? It's not as if she's the only girl in the world.

Abie: Yeah, Stu. There's *more* than *one fish* in the *sea*.

Stu: *(Sings.)*
>   There may be other fish in the sea,
>   But there's just one fish that I see,
>   And her name is Elemenope.
>   She's the fish for me!
>
>   Sure, there's Lisa and Liza,
>   There's Anna and Joanna.
>   But of all these fish,
>   Elemenope's the best dish.
>
>   There may be other cats in the batch,
>   But for me there's only one catch—
>   Elemenope's my one true match,
>   Elemenope lights my match.
>
>   There's Carrie and Sherrie,
>   There's Connie and Bonnie.
>   But of all these cats,

Ellie make's 'em look like rats.

A., C., & V.: *(Sing.)*
> Stu, there's other fish in the sea,
> And there's not just one fish for you.
> There are other girls than Elemenope.
> Try to make your horizons blue.
>
> Stu, there's Corrine and Dorrine,
> There's Abbie—

Abie: —And Abie!

A., C., & V.:
> Sure Elemenope's a nice dish,
> But she's not the only fish!

(Music ends. SEDIEFGE enters from the house with ELEMENOPE and HIGH JACK, who are hand in hand.)

Sediefge: *(Clearing his throat to get everyone's attention.)* Excuse me! Can I have everyone's attention please? *(As the PEASANTS begin to crowd around.)* I would like to make an announcement. As of this past half hour, I have found a suitor for my beautiful daughter Elemenope. *(Groans of despair emit forth from the MALE PEASANTS.)* I proudly introduce my future son-in-law, Sir Bruswayne. *(Pinching ELEME-NOPE'S glowing cheek.)* The two love-birds shall be leaving for Sir Bruswayne's home country first thing in the morning. *(More groans of despair from the MALE PEASANTS while the FEMALE PEASANTS applaud loudly.)* That is all. Good afternoon to you all.

High Jack: *(Bowing and taking ELEMENOPE'S hand.)* I shall see you in the morning, my turtle dove of love.

(ELEMENOPE giggles as SEDIEFGE and SHE return inside. HIGH JACK crosses to the group at the fountain.)

High Jack: *(To STU.)* Be at the dock an hour before sunrise. I shall sneak you on board and take you, with Elemenope, back to my home country with me.

Stu: *(Ecstatically.)* Sir, I thank you a thousand times! Thank you, thank you, thank you, thank you, thank you—

High Jack: *(Impatiently.)* All right!!! One thank you is more than enough. Be there or else you can forget about seeing her ever again.

(VIEW and HIGH JACK cross to U.R. and turn their backs to the audience. CURE crosses to U.L. and turns his back to the audience. ABIE pulls STU aside, music under.)

Stu: *(music under)* What is it, Abie?

Abie: *(Confidentially, music under)* Stu, I don't trust this "Sir Bruswayne." I know it sounds crazy, but I just can't help feeling like I've seen him before. I just can't place it.

Stu: Abie, you're right, it does sound crazy. As usual, you're worrying too much. Please don't worry. Everything will turn out fine.

(STU exits. ABIE sighs, then exits as well, leaving CURE on stage with HIGH JACK and VIEW.)

Mysterious Off-Stage Voice: Of course, you could always have her kidnapped by pirates…*(fading)*…pirates…pirates…pirates…

Cure: *(CURE getting an idea)* Of course! It's so obvious! *(Approaches HIGH JACK and VIEW.)* Excuse me, Sir Bruswayne, or should I call you "High Jack the Pirate?" *("Shock chord" music.)*

High Jack: *(Glaring at CURE.)* Why do you call me by that name?

View: Because that's your name, High—I mean Sir Bruswayne.

Cure: Come, come, High Jack. You really don't think that removing your eye patch is enough of a disguise to fool me, do you?

High Jack: Well, I figured that if glasses worked for Clark Kent, why not try it with an eye patch? *(Sticking a knife to CURE'S throat, music under)* Well, I guess we'll just have to decide what to do with you, now won't we?

Cure: *(Gulping, music under)* Now, don't get hasty. I'm not here to turn you in or anything. I'm just interested in a…business proposition. *(He pulls a sapphire necklace out of his satchel.)*

High Jack: *(Interested.)* Business, eh? I enjoy business.

20

(Blackout.)

At Rise: *(Nightfall. Music under action. The PEASANTS are all sleeping on the streets, STU at his place on the pedestal. Two figures, HIGH JACK and VIEW, creep through the shadows, stepping over snoring bodies. As they step over ABIE, she wakes up, but stays still. As they enter the house, ABIE gets up and creeps up to the house, hoping to see what's going on. After a few moments, HIGH JACK and VIEW, now in their pirate clothes, emerge from the house carrying ELEMENOPE, bound and gagged.)*

Abie: *(Making the connection, music under.)* High Jack the pirate!

High Jack: *(Music under.)* That's right.

Abie: *(A bit confused.)* But you only have one eye. Sir Bruswayne had two eyes, I'm sure.

High Jack: *(Lifting his eye patch.)* The eye patch is just for appearances.

Abie: *(Trying to wake everyone.)* Wake up! Come on! Somebody wake—

(ABIE'S cut off as HIGH JACK grabs her and covers her mouth with his hand.)

High Jack: *(Sneering at her.)* Not so fast, woman. *(To VIEW.)* View, leave the note on the door.

(VIEW scribbles a few notes on a piece of paper and then walks up to the doorstep. He pulls out a knife and as he pins the note to the door with the knife, he hits the door too hard and it falls to the ground with a crash, startling him. The PEASANTS all look up. When they realize what happened, they put their heads back down, trying to stifle their laughs while staying in character. While HIGH JACK, ABIE and ELEMENOPE shake their heads in shame, VIEW, a bit startled, smiles at the audience and tries to put the door back up. He gets it to stand in the doorway, then turns around and poses triumphantly. As he poses, it crashes back down, causing him to jump in surprise. He looks at the door one more time, then shrugs and runs off carrying ELEMENOPE while HIGH JACK drags ABIE off.)

(Blackout.)

(Morning music lights up the scene. The PEASANTS are beginning to wake up when, suddenly, XYZE'S scream pierces the early morning silence. As the PEASANTS look around confused, XYZE runs out into the street screaming.)

Xyze: She's gone! She's gone! They've taken her! She's gone! *(An awkward pause. Music. She repeats, louder this time.)* I said, She's gone! She's gone! They've taken her! She's gone! *(Another pause, music. She improvises.)* Oh where, oh where could my husband, *Sediefge*, be during such a horrible crises. *(Pause, music. Improvises, music under.)* Umm…Oh, I know! Silly me! I left him chained to the bed. *(Smiling at the AUDIENCE as she runs into the house, tripping over the broken door, music under.)* Be right back! *(She returns dragging a groggy SEDIEFGE out by the ears.)*

As I was saying, *(Over-dramatically)* she's gone! She's gone! They've taken her! She's gone!

(SEDIEFGE stubs his toe on the broken door as XYZE drags him out onto the doorstep.)

Sediefge: *(Still waking up.)* Uh…who's gone? Who's gone? Who's taken who? Who's gone? *(He turns around and looks at the door on the ground..)* Umm…Look! Some cretins knocked our door down!

(The PEASANTS all snicker.)

Xyze: *(Trying to get him back on track.)* That isn't all that they've done! They've kidnapped Elemenope as well!

Sediefge and Peasant Men: *(music under)* No!!!!

(CURE, the only male not affected by the news, interrupts their keening.)

Cure: Sediefge! I believe that there is a ransom note pinned to your door. *(Out of habit, he points at the empty doorway. When he realizes the door is gone, he quickly points down at the door on the ground. SEDIEFGE runs to the door and grabs the note.)*

Sediefge: *(Reading aloud.)* "Greetings ladies and gentlemen, I regret to inform you that I have decided to kidnap the beautiful young maiden Elemenope. If you ever want to see her again…too bad, because this is not a ransom note. I hope with all sincerity that I have not caused too much inconvenience. With love, High Jack the Pirate. P.S.—We also kidnapped some peasant girl as well. Have a nice day, now." *(Tearing the note apart, screaming in rage.)* High Jack!!! Listen up all of you, and listen well! I will offer a reward of any price, anything, to the man who returns Elemenope to me, along with High Jack the Pirate stuck like a pig!

(With that, SEDIEFGE storms into the house, with XYZE following behind him, wailing in remorse. As they walk over the threshold, they trip over the broken door.)

Stu: *(Groaning in agony.)* Why God? What did I do to deserve such suffering?

Cure: Come now, Stu. What are you so upset about?

Stu: *(In disbelief.)* What am I so upset about? All is lost! I'll never see Elemenope again in my life.

Cure: *(Slapping him over the back.)* All is not lost my friend, all is better than you could ask for.

Stu: *(Hesitantly.)* What do you mean?

Cure: Simple, we can track down High Jack's camp, it can't be too hard to find him. After all, there *are* only seven seas. When we find his camp, we'll rescue Elemenope and you can claim your priceless reward: Elemenope's hand in marriage!

Stu: *(Jumping up ecstatically, sings.)*
       Cure, you're brilliant,
       You really are!
       You're so resilient,
       You're such a star!

Who would believe
(Tapping at CURE'S head.)
The wonders in there?
It's hard to conceive
How anyone can compare!

I'll save my girl,
I'll save the day!
I'll take no pearl,
I'll have my way!

I'll go to the end of the world for her!
Fight any pirate, slay any demon!
I'll go anywhere, hire any voyager!
Sail any ocean, climb any mountain!

I will not rest,
I will not sleep,
Until at last
I've saved my sheep!

All will be well,
All will be fine,
As soon as I'm
With my ma'moiselle!

I'll go to the end of the world for her!
Win any obstacle, climb any barrier.
I'll not give up, I will not deter
Until at long last I can carry her
Home!
I'll go to the end for her!

(Loud cackling can be heard coming from the crowd. TUTHRIE emerges from the crowd, a GIRL around each arm, laughing hysterically.)

Tuthrie: You're going to find High Jack's camp! That's a laugh! Ha! Tell me, have either of you ever even set foot on the sea? *(CURE and STU shake their heads.)* Then how do you expect to find his camp without a scrap of sea brains? *(Stupefied looks from STU and CURE.)* Well, you boys are in luck, because Old Tuthrie is gonna give you a helping hand. You see, before I retired as a pirate, I sailed the seven seas with High Jack, and I could take you to his camp, for the right price of course.

Stu: *(Overjoyed.)* Anything you want will be yours Tuthrie, anything. You ask and it will be yours!

Cure: *(Remaining calm and cool.)* Tuthrie, why on earth did you retire as a pirate, if you don't mind my asking.

Tuthrie: *(Confidentially, while covering the GIRLS' ears, music under.)* You see, I did it for the ladi[*].

Stu: *(Confused, music under.)* Ladi?

Tuthrie: *(matter-of-factly)* You know, plural ladies.
> *(Letting go of the GIRLS, he sings.)*
> As a pirate, I tried to get me girls,
> Pretty girls with pretty curls.
> Women very often flock to men—
> Men who live off of danger.

---

[*] Pronounced *lay-die*.

26

But despite the danger and adventures
It was still hard,
(Smiling)
even without no dentures.
Guess the raping and the pillaging,
Must have been what sent them running.

And then it hit me!
That's when I thought,
A pirate who used to be
Still has fought!

A pirate who has seen the light,
A pirate who's reformed to good,
Will still have fought the fight
And still be filled with livelihood.

That is how you win the girls,
Even the ones with the pretty curls.
So give her some fun and some danger
And soon you won't be a stranger.

All Men: *(Sing.)*
That is how you win the girls,
Not with diamonds or with pearls.
Don't woo 'em or please 'em
Or wine 'em or dine 'em,
Just tease 'em
With what you were!
That is how you win the girls!

(Blackout.)

Scene Change: *(The STATUE gets off the pedestal and a mock boat is put in its place. The top of the pedestal rocks back and forth, making the boat look like it's bobbing in the waves. Mechanical noises are coming from the pedestal, indicating the use of machinery to move its top.)*

At Rise: *(STU, CURE and TUTHRIE have set off on their voyage. TUTHRIE is standing at the wheel, breathing in the fresh sea air while CURE plays card solitaire and STU vomits over the side of the boat.)*

Mysterious Off-Stage Voice: And so the foolish threesome set off on their dangerous journey. Through the storms, sharks and seasickness, they pressed on toward their goal of High Jack's secret camp.

Stu: *(Coming up for a breath, music under.)* Are we almost there yet?

Tuthrie: *(Laughing uproariously, music under.)* Don't be silly, lad! We've only been at sea ten minutes! Me hopes you didn't have too big a breakfast; it looks like it's gonna be a choppy trip!

Cure: *(Music under.)* Hey, I won!

(At that, the mechanical noises sputter and the pedestal comes to a stop. An awkward pause. The three look at each other, unable to figure out what to do.)

MOSV: Well come on, you idiots! Grab some oars and start rowing.

(Shrugging, STU and CURE grab imaginary oars and - smiling at the audience - begin "rowing" the boat while humming "The Show Must Go On.")

Tuthrie: *(As CURE and STU attempt rowing, in different directions)* Together...together...together... *(etc...)*

(Blackout as SINGERS cut off after a few verses. Music continues through remaining scene change.)

Scene Change: *(The boat is removed and a lawn chair rests on the pedestal, serving as HIGH JACK'S throne. The balcony railing is removed along with the doorstep, door and any other decorations on SEDIEFGE'S house. It should now just be a blank object, which serves as a hill or some such landmass, which some of the pirates sit on, dangling their legs over the side.)*

At Rise: *(HIGH JACK'S camp. The PIRATE'S are all sitting around cheering as the DANCER GIRLS put on a dance show for them. HIGH JACK is relaxing on his throne, being fanned by two women while he sips through a straw out of a lemonade glass with a mini-umbrella.)*

Pirates: *(Sing, while one DANCER GIRL steps forward and dances, swaying her hips seductively.)*
      Look at those hips,
(The DANCER GIRL smiles provocatively.)
      Look at those lips!
      Watch her dance now,
      Dance for us, darlin'!

(The DANCER GIRL performs a dance solo, the PIRATES cheering her on. She finishes, blowing a kiss to the PIRATES. Another DANCER GIRL, with legs that go ALL the way up, steps forward and begins dancing.)

Pirates: *(sing)*
      Look at those legs!
(To VIEW)
      Go get more kegs!
(He runs off.)
      Watch her dance now,
      Dance for us, darlin'!

(The DANCER GIRL performs a dance solo, the PIRATES "oohing" and "aahing." VIEW returns, stumbling as he carries a keg that is way too heavy for him.)

Pirates: *(sing)*
>The life of a pirate gets awful lonely.
>It sure is nice to come home
>To some lovely non-homely
>Women from Rome!

(A well-endowed DANCER GIRL steps forward and begins dancing.)

Pirates: *(sing)*
>Look at that chest!
>This is the best!
>Watch her dance now,
>Dance for us, darlin'!

(The DANCER GIRL performs a dance solo, the PIRATES hooting and hollering. End music.)

High Jack: *(Yawning.)* Bring out the new girls!

View: But High Jack, our employer gave us strict orders to leave the girls alone. He wouldn't like it if he found out we had them dancing for the—

High Jack: *(Sneering at VIEW.)* View, the *employer* isn't here, now is he?

View: *(Gulping.)* No, High Jack.

High Jack: Then he'll never know, now will he?

View: No, High Jack.

(Two PIRATES drag ELEMENOPE and ABIE out onto stage. ELEMENOPE, as usual, is nothing but bright,

cheery smiles. ABIE, on the other hand, is significantly less perky.)

Elemenope: *(Sings.)*
　　　My father always told me smile
　　　No matter what.
　　　Whatever happens don't lose your guile,
　　　It's what you've got.

　　　For a smile can go a long, long way,
　　　A smile can change another person's day.
(smile growing.)
　　　So I smile, and I smile, and I smile, and I smile
　　　All the whole long while.

Abie: *(sings, simultaneously with above.)*
　　　She's always smiling
　　　No matter what
　　　What is with this never-ending
　　　Felicity?

　　　Here we are kidnapped and far away,
　　　Nothing but wenches for their play,
(Mimicking ELEMENOPE.)
　　　Still she smiles, and she smiles,
　　　and she smiles, and she smiles.
　　　My God, how she smiles.

(During this, three new DANCER GIRLS - STU, CURE and TUTHRIE in disguise - enter the scene. They sneakily approach THREE PASSED-OUT PIRATES and take their weapons. As ELEMENOPE and ABIE finish singing and the PIRATES applaud, STU, CURE and TUTHRIE jump in front of ELEMENOPE and ABIE, wielding their swords to the PIRATES.)

Stu: (*Speaks, music under.*) Fear not, ladies, for we have come to save the day!

High Jack: (*Looking at them strangely. Speaks, music under.*) Not if we have anything to say about it!

Cure: (*Speaks, music under.*) We aren't leaving without the women.

High Jack: Then prepare for a fight! Pirates, charge!

(*Music ends.*)

View: But High Jack, it's un-gentlemanly to fight women.

High Jack: They're not women, you idiot! They're men in drag!

View: (*Eyeing TUTHRIE impishly.*) I don't know, this one looks too pretty to be a man.

Tuthrie: (*Growling.*) Back off, shrimpy. We don't play that game here.

View: (*Cowering away.*) Okay, she's a he! Pirate's charge!

(*A battle ensues. STU and HIGH JACK duel. STU lunges triumphantly and suddenly a look of surprise spreads across HIGH JACK'S face as STU defeats him, running his sword into him.*)

High Jack: (*In shock, music under.*) You stabbed me!

Stu: *(Confused, music under.)* What are you talking about? Of course I stabbed you, it's in the script.

High Jack: No, you actually stabbed me. *(A look of terror spreads over STU'S face.)* No, don't worry about me—the show must go on!

Company: *(Dancing around HIGH JACK, who's lying on the ground, holding his stomach, they sing.)*
>Here in the theater,
>An'thing can go wrong.
>It doesn't matter,
>The show must go on!
>
>Stabbings or muggings,
>Jabbings or thuggings,
>Still doesn't matter
>The show must go on!
>
>Sandbags may fall,
>Set parts may break,
>Cupid may call
>During an earthquake!
>
>Actors may miss cues,
>Taking a quick snooze.
>Whatever goes wrong,
>The show must go on!
>The show must go on!

Cure: *(Speaks, music under.)*[4] After intermission!
End of Act I.

---

[4] Same as before, if the audience applauds, cut them off and scold them. If they don't applaud at the end of the song, tell them they can now. If they didn't hold their applause at the start of the show and they do this time, congratulate them. Etc.

34

Act II

(The scene has frozen where we left off, with STU standing over the corpse of HIGH JACK, who has been replaced by a mannequin, and the other PIRATES in various combat poses. The ACTOR playing CURE steps out of the portrait and confronts the AUDIENCE.)

Cure: Welcome back! I'm glad you all returned despite that rather...eventful first act. We here at *(name of theater or production company)* constantly strive to bring you, the theater-goer, the absolute best in theatrical quality. Other productions may use props and gimmicks, but *we* use *real* blood! The directors just wanted me to inform you that the actor playing High Jack is just fine and is expected back from the E.R. in time for curtain call. I promise you that the second act of our performance shall not be nearly as eventful as the first act. *(Pauses, thinking about what he just said.)* I meant that in a good way. And now...Act II!

(CURE steps back into the portrait and the scene unfreezes. With the death of their leader, the other PIRATES flee chaotically. TUTHRIE, enjoying himself, teases some of the lost PIRATES by poking them and chasing them. He eventually chases one off U.L.)

Abie: *(Overjoyed, trying to jump into STU'S arms.)* Stu! I knew you'd come for me!

(But STU, who is preoccupied with ELEMENOPE, doesn't catch her and she plops to the ground. STU and ELEMENOPE stare at each other for one of those sweet little moments. Nice little love music plays softly.)

Abie: *(Sings bitterly.)*
>"Oh, how are you, Abie?"
>Oh, I'm alright.
>"Did they hurt you, or fill your heart with
>>fright?"
>Don't be silly.
>
>Really Stu,
>I really am fine.
>Really I'm…
>I'm Really…fine.

(STU and ELEMENOPE begin an abstract waltz as ABIE and CURE—the latter rather menacingly—watch on.)

Abie: *(sings)*
>There he is
>Going on and living on
>Not caring how I care for him
>Not seeing how *I* can't go on.
>
>There he is
>Loving on and moving on
>Not seeing how I look at him
>Not caring that *I* can't move on.
>
>His gentle smile
>Warms my heart all the while
>His lovely eyes
>Makes my soul start to rise.
>
>There he is
>Loving her and not me

He drives a dagger through my heart
Which tares my life and soul apart.

There he is
Standing right over there
Going on without a care
Not even seeing me here.

You know, I guess it's true
What people say,
That none of us can help
Where we fall in love.

(Nice little love music continues.)

Stu: I'm Stu.

Elemenope: *(Smiling densely, as she breaks the moment, and the music.)* I'm Elemenope, I smile a lot.

Stu: We've come to rescue you.

(TUTHRIE runs in from U.L., breathing heavily.)

Tuthrie: The pirates sank our ship!

Abie: *(Lashing out.)* Why? What did I ever do to deserve this?

Elemenope: Cheer up, Abbie. Put on a happy smile.

Abie: *(Approaching ELEMENOPE menacingly.)* My name is—

37

(Suddenly, a phone begins ringing. The CONDUCTOR pulls out his cell phone.)

Conductor: *(To CAST.)* Sorry, this will be just a second. *(Into phone.)* Hello? Oh hi, Tony. Gee, how have you been? How's Maria and the kids? Oh me, nothing much. Just doing some conducting gig. Yeah, that's the one. Well, what can I say? It's not *Boheme* but on the other hand, it's not *Cats* either, so I guess I shouldn't complain too much. Hey listen, it's been great talking to you, but I should probably get back to work here. Yeah, you too. Hey, call me sometime tomorrow night and we'll figure out some time to get together for dinner. Whoa, now. Caroline's stopped drinking since that incident and she promises that she won't let it happen next time we come over. Okay, well I gotta go. Talk to you tomorrow night. Naw, don't worry about interrupting the show. Okay, later bubby. *(To CAST, putting away his cell phone.)* You may proceed.

Abie: *(Dumb-struck.)* Uhh…okay…*(Picking up where she left off.)* My name is—

Elemenope: Really, Abbie. You shouldn't be so over-dramatic.

Abie: *(over-dramatically)* As God is my witness, I AM NOT OVER-DRAMATIC!

Tuthrie: *(Cutting in.)* Okay, now don't get me wrong here, I love a cat fight just as much as the next guy, but if you two would let me finish my sentences you'd know that I had some good news. You see, since High Jack was the only pirate who could sail, the other pirates have spread out all over the island, abandoning their ship. *(Eyeing a box of treasure left at the base of HIGH JACK'S throne.)* And my, my! They left their booty as well! I suppose that this will be enough payment for my troubles—*(Eyeing the DANCER GIRLS.)*—along with these beautiful ladies. *(He leads the DANCER GIRLS off.)* You know, ladies, I once was a pirate, but I have since seen the light and reformed my ways!

(As the DANCER GIRLS ooh, aah, and giggle over him, he flashes a knowing smile at STU and CURE. STU lifts the treasure box and follows after him, followed by ABIE. CURE and ELEMENOPIE are the last to leave. CURE, for once, seems somewhat disappointed.)

(Blackout.)

Scene Change: *(The same boat can be used for this voyage, but a pirate flag should be added. The machine appears to have been fixed during intermission.)*

At Rise: *(The PARTY has set off, once again, on their voyage. TUTHRIE stands proudly at the wheel, the DANCER GIRLS hanging on him, running their hands through his hair; ELEMENOPE and CURE are playing an intense game of cards, ELEMENOPE smiling ever-after, CURE a bit moody; and ABIE and STU are vomiting over the side.)*

Mysterious Off-Stage Voice: And so the foolish orgy set off, *again*, on their dangerous journey across the sea.

Elemenope: *(Jumping ecstatically.)* Yay! You won!

39

(Once again, the machine breaks down and the frustrated ENSEMBLE pull out real oars—a precaution taken after the first-act incident—and begin rowing and humming "The Show Must Go On," mumbling curses at the tech crew.)

Tuthrie: *(Trying to get the group to row in the same direction.)* Together...together...together...together... *(etc...)*

(Blackout as SINGERS cut off after a few verses. Music continues through remaining scene change.)

Scene Change: *(The boat is removed and the STATUE takes its place. SEDIEFGE'S house has returned to normal, with the exception of the broken door which has since been dragged off-stage.)*

At Rise: *(At long last, CURE, ELEMENOPE, STU, ABIE, and TUTHRIE, along with the DANCER GIRLS, have returned home. They are warmly welcomed by the PEASANTS.)*

PEASANTS: *(sing)*
> Oh, happy day!
> Oh, happy, happy day!
> At long, long, last
> Our friends have returned home,
> The danger's past!
>
> Oh, happy day!
> Oh, happy, sappy day!
> Our fears are gone,
> We have no need to fawn!

The darkness has withdrawn!

Sound the choir bells,
Sing it from the chapels,
After voyage and battle,
Cure and friends have brought home Sediefge's
    chattel,
Our beloved and oh, so lovely Elemenope!

Abie: *(calling out, jumping up and down, but ignored)*
   And Abie!!!!

PEASANTS: *(continuing)*
   This is surely news that'll
   Bring tears of joy to our little
   Town!

(ELEMENOPE'S parents burst out of their house and deliver a thousand hugs and kisses to her. Literally. She eventually has to pry them off of her so that she can breathe.)

Sediefge: *(sings)*
   Oh, thank heaven! PEASANTS: *(sing)*
              Hooray!

Xyze: *(sings)*
   Oh, praise the Lord!

           Hurrah!

Sediefge:
   Are you all right, my cactus wren?
           Happy day!

Xyze: Did you see a fjord?

41

Hur…huh?

Sediefge:

    Did they touch you?

Happy, happy, joy, joy
Happy, happy joy!

Xyze: Was there much you…   *(etc.)*

Sediefge:

    Rest assured…

Xyze: …Endured while you toured?

Sediefge:

    …My little prairie dog…

Xyze: Did you get lost in a bog?

Sediefge:

    …I'll never, ever, never…

Xyze: We thought we lost you forever!

Sediefge:

    …Lose you ever again!

Xyze: *(to SEDIEFGE)*

    Did you call her a cactus wren?

Sediefge:

    At last we can say "amen!"

Xyze: What the hell's a cactus wren?

Sediefge:

    A type of wren, of course!

42

Sediefge and Xyze:
> Oh, my dear, my pet, we're just so glad,
> We have no more need for remorse,
> For nevermore will our days be sad.

Sediefge, Xyze, PEASANTS:
> This day shall go down in an historical tome,
> For finally,
> At long, long last,
> Our dearest, most beloved,
> Beautiful and oh so lovely Elemenope...

Abie: *(calling out jumping up and down, still ignored)*
> And Abie!!!!

Sediefge, Xyze, PEASANTS:
> ...Has returned home!!!!!

Sediefge *(spoken)*: Who is the hero who has rescued my beloved daughter from the barbarians?

Stu: *(Stepping forward.)* It was I, sir. Along with my friends Cure and Tuthrie.

Sediefge: *(Shaking their hands.)* I thank you a thousand times! Thank you, thank you, thank you, thank you, thank you, thank you, thank you—

Company: Enough!

Sediefge: *(Embarrassed.)* Sorry. Now, what do you valiant men want for your reward?

Cure: *(Stepping forward.)* I, sir, have no interest nor desire for material possessions, but I believe that my partners do.

Tuthrie: *(Stepping forward, DANCER GIRLS hanging on him.)* I, too sir, have all that I could possibly want for the time being. *(Jingles his purse of pirate loot and smiles at the GIRLS as they gawk over him.)*

Sediefge: *(To STU.)* And you, sir? I suppose you want no reward, either.

Stu: No, sir. *(Takes a deep breath.)* I would like to ask you, sir, for your daughter's hand in marriage.

(As SEDIEFGE'S face turns sixteen shades of red, TUTHRIE pulls a shapphire bracelet, the same sapphire bracelet CURE gave to HIGH JACK, out of his purse and slyly hands it to STU. STU then pretends as if he is taking the bracelet out of his purse. SEDIEFGE is distracted.)

Stu: *(music under)* I would be more than willing to offer a gift to the family as a sign of friendship.

Sediefge: *(Sings, in a trance.)*
      Sapphires!
      Oh, how I love my sapphires!
      Oh, how I love my worldly objects
      With optical attraction!

      See how they sparkle,
      See how they twinkle!
      Oh, how I love my sapphires!
      Oh, how I love my jewels!

44

(SEDIEFGE continues to drool over the bracelet as XYZE steps forward.)

Xyze: *(Sings)*
> Watch how that disgustin' slob drools,
> Over his precious jewels.
> God, it makes me sick,
> When I look at the man I chose to pick.
>
> Sure, there was a time
> When he was young an' han'some.
> But, now I wouldn't pay a dime,
> Not a cent of ransom.
>
> Look at him now,
> Always playing with his jewels.
> The man would rather rub his jewels
> Than play with his frau.

Sediefge: *(Speaks, grabbing the bracelet from STU.)* Of course, you may take my daughter's hand in marriage. No matter what his position in life, any man who has the courage to rescue my daughter from pirates is certainly a worthy suitor. And if he has pretty jewels, even better!

Stu: *(Not quite believing his ears.)* Thank you, sir. *(To ELEMENOPE.)* Elemenope, will you take my hand in marriage?

Elemenope: *(Smiling enthusiastically.)* Of course I will!

Cure: *(Dumb-struck.)* Uhh...is that your *final* answer?

Sediefge: Wonderful news! I invite you all into my home to celebrate this joyous occasion.

(The CROWD cheers and everyone enters the house except CURE, STU and ELEMENOPE.)

Elemenope: *(Kissing STU lightly on the cheek.)* I'll be right in, you go on ahead.

Stu: *(In a dream world.)* Very well, I'll see you inside. *(He enters the house. ELEMENOPE crosses to CURE.)*

Elemenope: Cure, do you think that we should tell everyone about our engagement *before* I get married to Stu or *after*?

Cure: *(Looking at her unbelievingly.)* Probably before. It wasn't supposed to be this complicated in the first place. High Jack wasn't supposed to lose the fight, I paid him to win! With Stu gone, it was supposed to be just you and me. But now, look at what's happened.

Elemenope: But do you think we should say something.

(CURE looks at her a moment, then replies.)

Cure: Yes. I'll talk to Stu first chance I get. Don't worry, it won't get any worse.

(They walk inside the house. As they disappear inside, ABIE climbs out from behind the pedestal, burdened with this new information.)

Abie: What do I do?

Mysterious Off-Stage Voice: Tell him, duh.

Abie: But, if I tell him, then he'll be heart-broken.

M.O.S.V.: Won't his heart be broken anyway?

Abie: Well…yes, but…

M.O.S.V.: Then tell him.

Abie: Wait a minute…who *are* you, anyway?

M.O.S.V.: Me? Oh…umm…well I AM THE MYS-TERIOUS OFF-STAGE VOICE… *(fading)* VOICe… VOIce…VOice…voice…

Abie: I see…But how do I tell him?

M.O.S.V.: 'Fraid I can't help you there.

Abie: Great. Some third-person narrator *you* make.

M.O.S.V.: I never claimed to be omniscient. Geez. Everyone thinks that just because I'm a mysteriously disembodied voice that I have the answer to everything. "Gee, Mr. Mysterious Off-Stage Voice, my wife doesn't love me anymore, what should I do?" "Shucks, Mr. Mysterious Off-Stage Voice, I want to become a professional millionaire, how can I do that?" "¿Vainas, Señor Misterioso fuera del Escenario Voz, pienso que quiero joder a un puerco espín, que es una idea buena?" Well you know what? I don't have the answer to everything! So maybe you should figure things out for yourself.

Abie: Sorry…I guess I should…
(Sings.)
How do I tell him?
How do I tell him?
I have to tell him,
Don't I?

What can I do?
There must be something.
Anything?
Just one clue?

I will tell him,
Though it will be grim.
I have to do it,
Though he'll have a fit.

I'll go to the end of the world for him!
Though he may not care, I'll stand by him.
I'll fight it out through thick and thin!
Go anywhere, my love is genuine.

I will not rest,
I'll sing no hymn,
Until at last,
I've said to him,

"She loves you not,
She'll bring you cries.
Open your eyes,
I'm what you've got!"

I'll go to the end of the world for Stu!
No matter how hard, I swear I will pursue!

I'll do anything, be his heroine,
Until he at last sees me as I see him!
I'll go to the end for him!

(Blackout.)

At Rise: *(At L., ELEMENOPE sits in front of her mirror powdering herself while reciting instructions to her parents for the wedding day. At R., STU, CURE and ABIE stand frozen in darkness.)*

Elemenope: *(sings)*
> We'll need flowers.

Sediefge: *(sings)*
> Flowers?

Xyze: *(sings)*
> Flowers.

Elemenope:
> Preferably petulias.

Sediefge:
> Petulias?

Elemenope:
> Petulias.

Sediefge:
> Sounds expensive.

Elemenope:
> Father!

Xyze: I think she means petunias.

Sediefge: *(To XYZE, indicating ELEMENOPE.)*
        No need to get defensive!
(To ELMENOPE.)
        Why not settle for gilliflowers?
(Receives glares from ELEMENOPE and XYZE.)
        I'll call the florist, Julius.

Elemenope:
        I'll need a wedding vower…

Sediefge:
        A wedding vower?

Elemenope:
        To write my wedding vows.
        I'm sure there's a web-site I can browse…

Sediefge:
        How much do you think it will cost?

Xyze: Dear!

Sediefge:
        I just don't want our fortune lost!

Elemenope:
        Could we have a baboon embossed?

(Lights dim on ELEMENOPE, SEDIEFGE, and XYZE and come up on CURE, ABIE and STU. STU is pacing frantically, not paying attention to ABIE and CURE.)

Abie: *(sings)*
        Stu—

Cure: *(sings)*
        Stu—

Abie: —I need to tell you—

Cure: —There's something I need to tell you—

Abie –I think that you should know—

Cure: —I don't think you want to—

Together:
        —Don't listen to him/her, listen to me!
        This is important!

Cure: You see—

Abie: You see—

Cure: —There is this little problem—

Abie: —I think you have a problem—

Cure: —With marrying Elemenope—

Abie: —You cant marry Elemenope—

Cure: —One of us can't—

Abie: —You really can't.
        Stu—

51

Cure: Stu—

Abie: —There's something I need to tell you—

Cure: —There's something you should know—

Abie: —You see—

Cure: —There's something I need to tell you—

Abie: —There's something you should know—

Cure: —You see—

Abie: —There is this little problem—

Cure: —You can't marry Elemenope!

Abie: —With marrying Elemenope!

Together:
>Don't listen to her/him, listen to me!
>This is important!

Stu: *(Exploding.)* WHAT???!!!

(An awkward pause.)

Cure: *(To ABIE.)*
>You go first.

(STU, fed up, storms away as they argue.)

Abie: No, you go first.

Cure: I insist.

Abie: I really can't!

Cure: I gotta piss,
So I t'ink I'll go tinkle.

Abie: You can hold it
While I withhold it...
(CURE looks at her oddly, clearly having misunderstood)
What I need to tell him, I mean...

(Lights fade on them and come up on ELEMENOPE, SEDIEFGE and XYZE.)

Elemenope:
I'll need a dress and a veil.

Sediefge:
What a mess!

Xyze: *(Browsing through a wedding catalog)*
Ooh look, a sale!

Elemenope:
We'll need a cake and some swans.

Sediefge:
Instead of a cake, how about won-tons?
(Receives glares from the women, again.)
Guess I can't fool yas.

(A FLORIST enters with a bouquet of petunias.)

Xyze:
> Here come the petulias—
> I mean the petunias.

Elemenope: *(Running to the FLORIST.)*
> Ooh, oh yay!

Sediefge: *(Looking at the long bill the FLORIST hands him, and handing the FLORIST some cash.)*
> *This* is the bill?

Elemenope: *(As the FLORIST walks away.)*
> What's that smell?

Xyze: *(Smelling the flowers.)*
> They smell kinda rotten.

Sediefge:
> What a bill for rotten petunias!

Elemenope:
> What have we forgotten?
> We got the shears and the spears...

Xyze: We got the maids with the braids...

Elemenope:
> For the party we got the stripper...

Xyze: What a hottie with what a dipper!

Elemenope:
> Mother!

Xyze: *(Blushing.)*
> Sorry. We got the feast…

Elemenope:
> Oh, I know, we forgot the priest!

Sediefge:
> Look at this bill!

(Blackout.)

(The wedding day. The town is bustling with the excitement of the big day. A DRUNKEN PRIEST is running around trying to get someone's attention, but no one pays him any notice.)

Priest: *(music under)* Excuse me! Can someone tell me who the bride and groom are?

Peasants: *(Sing.)*
> There's a wedding today,
> Hooray!
> There's a wedding today,
> Happy day!
>
> We'd best not be late for the wedding today!
> Such a momentous event this day will be!
> On this most joyous of happy days,
> Stu and Elemenope will be joined in matrimony
> At the wedding today!

(The PEASANTS scatter variously—some remain onstage, some run off and so-on through the remainder of the song.)

Priest: *(chasing after the scattering PEASANTS)* Excuse me! Hello!

(STU rushes on stage from L., looking for CURE.)

Stu: *(Sings.)*
> Where is Cure?
> He should be here!
> He's the best man after all!
> I'm the one who's s'posed to get cold feet,
> Not him!

(ABIE runs on and crosses to STU.)

Abie: *(Music under.)* Stu, there's something I need to tell you!

Stu: *(Sings.)*
> Abie, not now!
> Can't you see
> I'm getting married today?

Abie: *(Music under.)* But Stu, I have to warn you—

Stu: *(Sings.)*
> Abie, baby,
> Don't worry,
> Everything will be fine.
> Now if you don't mind,
> There's a wedding today…
> And it's mine!!!

(STU runs off and ABIE runs after him, trying to get him to pay attention to her. The PRIEST runs on and sees them running off.)

Priest: *(running after them)* Excuse me! Sir! Miss!

(ELEMENOPE runs on, fussing with her hair.)

Elemenope: *(Sings.)*
> My hair! My Hair!
> Just look at my hair!
> I want it to go right, but it goes left!
> I want it to curl, but it goes straight!
> *(Tugging on her hair.)*
> I have a wedding today,
> And I'll look like a parrot!

(ELEMENOPE runs off. The PRIEST comes on and sees her running off, he chases after her.)

Priest: Excuse me young lady!

(XYZE and SEDIEFGE enter. XYZE is trying to tie SEDIEFGE'S tie while SEDIEFGE spouts off.)

Sediefge: *(Sings.)*	Xyze: *(Sings.)*
But dear, don't you agree?	Yes, dear.
I mean, we have to stick	
To our principles.	Of course we do, dear.
The lower class doesn't marry	
The upper class.	Hold still!
That's just how it is!	You're absolutely right, dear.

Sediefge: *(Speaks, music under.)* Those are the rules and the rules, and the rules are not broken! He does, though, have lovely jewels...

(XYZE drags him off by his tie as the PRIEST enters and sees them leaving.)

Priest: *(running after them)* Hey! Come back here!

(CURE enters.)

Cure: *(Sings.)*
>How do I tell him?
>How do I tell him?
>I have to tell him,
>Don't I?
>
>It won't be easy, that's for sure.
>I mean, I only tried to have him killed by pirates,
>So what?
>I'm sure that years from now
>We'll look back at this and laugh!

(Strains laughing.)
>See, I'm laughing already!

(STU runs on, ABIE following close behind him.)

Stu: *(Music under.)* Cure, there you are! I've been looking everywhere for you! Come, we must go.

(STU starts to drag CURE off by the collar.)

Cure: *(Gagging, music under.)* Wait! Stu, there's something I need to tell you.

Stu: *(Sings.)*
>Cure, Abie,
>Don't worry,

Everything will be fine.
Now if you don't mind,
There's a wedding today…
And it's mine!

(The COMPANY enters.)

Stu: Elemenope:
   Cure, Abie,   My hair! My hair!
   Don't worry,   Just look at my hair!
   Everything will be   I want it to go right,
       fine.   but it goes left!
   Now if you don't   I want it to curl, but it goes
       mind,   straight!
   There's a wedding   I have a wedding today,
       today,
   And it's mine!   And I'll look like a parrot!

Sediefge: *(simult. with above.)*   Xyze:
   But dear, don't you agree?   Yes, dear.
   I mean, we have to stick
   To our principles.   Of course we do,
         dear.

   The lower class does not marry
   The upper class.   Hold still!
   That's just how it is!   You're absolutely
         right, dear.

Cure: *(simultaneously with above.)*   Abie:
   It won't be easy, that's for   How do I tell him?
      sure.
   I mean, I only tried to have   How do I tell him?
   him killed by pirates,   I have to tell him,
   So what?   Don't I?
   I'm sure that years from now   It won't be easy,
         that's for sure.

   We'll look back at this   But somehow I

and laugh!   know I
(Strains laughing.)
    See, I'm laughing already!   Have to tell Stu!

Peasants: *(simultaneously with above [optional])*
    There's a wedding today,
    Hooray!
    There's a wedding today,
    Happy day!
    We best not be late for the wedding today!
    Such a momentous event this day will be!

(The PRIEST, losing patience, screams out.)

Priest: Could someone please tell me who the hell the bride and groom are?

(Silence. The PRIEST blushes and crosses himself.)

Priest: *(Meekly.)* Sorry, Lord.

(STU and ELEMENOPE step forward.)

Priest: *(Sweetly.)* Aaw, what another lovely couple. *(Cutting the sweet stuff, taking a sip of brandy.)* All right, let's get this over with. I have two more romantic slaps in the face to conduct today. First of all, if there is anyone here who opposes this union, please step forward now or forever hold your tongue blah, blah, blah, yackity-smackity. *(Not even bothering to pause.)* Good. Now—

Cure: Uh, I oppose this union, Father.

(At that, a sandbag falls from the loft to the stage. After an awkward pause the PRIEST looks at CURE awkwardly for a moment, then shrugs.)

Priest: *(improvising)* Well, there's a first time for everything.

(CURE turns to the guests and explains.)

Cure: You see, Elemenope and I have been engaged for several months now. We kept our engagement a secret because we knew Sediefge would oppose. We were waiting for an opportunity to run away and elope.

(SEDIEFGE rises, turning sixteen shades of red.)

Xyze: Oh, you better not have touched her knippel, mister!

Cure: I have another confession to make. I was born into a wealthy family. My parents were very rich and spoiled me as a child. When I became a teenager, I grew to resent their lack of attention towards me, so I ran away from home and moved to the streets, bringing a few family jewels with me. I gave some of the jewels to High Jack to kidnap Elemenope. I gave some more jewels to Tuthrie to lead Stu and me to High Jack's camp, where High Jack was supposed to–

(Suddenly, HIGH JACK and VIEW burst in on the scene. HIGH JACK is very clearly heavily drugged with some perfectly decent pain-killers. He is heavily bandaged and his arm is in a sling. VIEW has a band-aid on his forehead.)

High Jack: I object!!!

View: Yeah, he objects.

Priest: Take a number.

Abie: High Jack the Pirate! But you're dead!

High Jack: Not as dead as you would think, it would seem! Did any of you think to check my pulse? No! Fortunately, View here is certified in CPR – it's a requirement I ask of any first mate when hiring – and he was able to nurse me back to health. This wedding is a sham! *(pointing at ELEMENOPE)* That girl is the rightful property of myself and my band of scallywags, rapists, and murderers.

View: I try to stay away from the murderers, they give me the heebie-jeebies.

High Jack: *(pointing at CURE)* That man paid me to kidnap the girl and kill the boy *(indicating STU)* when they came to rescue her so that he *(indicating CURE)* could run off with her *(indicating ELEMENOPE)*. Considering the pain, suffering and neglect I had to go through, I consider the latter part of the deal void and therefore Elemenope is my rightful property to do with as I please.

View: *(to ELEMENOPE)* Usually what pleases him is a good game of *Monopoly*.

Abie: Are you telling me that you came back all this way just for her? I mean, yeah she's pretty but she's dumber than a dumpster and as annoying as a myna bird.

Elemenope: *(touched, near tears)* Abie, I didn't know you felt that way. You are too sweet.

High Jack: No, that is not all I came back for. I came back to settle another indignity that has been besought upon my character. I want a song.

COMPANY: *(confused)* What?

High Jack: I am the only character in this silly play, *(to PRIEST)* with the exception of your holiness of course, who doesn't get a song. I want a damn song!
        (sings)
        What is the theater coming to today,
        When the most handsome, brilliant, clever,
        Intelligent and oh, so humble
        Character in the show, doesn't get a song in the play?

View, Priest: *(sing)*
        Where's his song?

High Jack:
        What can we say about the state of the world,
        When the man who should be the star never
        Gets to sing or dance or rant or mumble
        When everyone else has tapped and twirled?

View, Priest:
        He should have a song!

63

High Jack:	View, Priest:
So right this wrong!	Ooh.
Bring justice to this day!	Aah.
And write my song	Ooh.
At the end of the play!	Aah.

View: Give him his damn	Priest: Give him his damn
Song!	– sorry, Lord – song!

High Jack:	Women:
Because I want a damn song!	Ooh…
Is that so wrong?	
I just want to sing and dance	
And maybe even prance!	

Alls I want's a grand song!
It won't have to be long.
And at the end of my unplanned song
I'm gonna get atop my boat
And rip off my Captain's coat!
I'll give the critics lines to quote
And all the groupie girls shall dote
Upon me!

I'll bring life to what the play-write wrote!
And bring the audience's souls afloat!
The sheep shall come out with the goats
Leaving the comfort of their cotes!
And the Gods upon their thrones, remote,
Shall weep like children as I emote
And sing a really long –

(HIGH JACK'S last note is cut off as CURE hits him over the head with the fallen sandbag. HIGH JACK collapses to the stage.)

64

Cure: Sorry, but that was getting annoying.

View: *(nervously as everyone turns to stare at him)* Well, hehe, I guess we'll be going then! *(he bends down to help HIGH JACK up)* Come on High Jack, we better get going before the nice villagers lynch us like at the last singing town we raided...

High Jack: *(groggily getting to his feet)* Did I sing a song, mommy?

View: Yes, High Jack, you sang a song...

(VIEW quickly leads a limping HIGH JACK off-stage and away from the angry PEASANTS.)

Elemenope: Cure, why didn't you tell me you had money?

Cure: I didn't want you to look at me that way. I wanted you to love me for me, not my inheritance. I truly apologize to everyone for all the inconvenience—

Policeman: *(From behind the audience.)* Stop the show!

(Three POLICEMEN march down the aisles and up on stage, much to the frustration of the actors.)

Policeman: *(Pointing at TUTHRIE, who is hiding behind his DANCER GIRLS.)* That man! You, sir, must come with us!

Cure: *(Stepping between the POLICEMEN and TUTHRIE.)* Excuse me, officer, but what is this all about.

Policeman: *(Pointing at TUTHRIE.)* We found illegal substances in the back of that man's garage.

Tuthrie: Oops.

Cure: Illegal substances? What kind of illegal substances?

Policeman: Jamaican squash.

Stu: Jamaican squash? What the hell is Jamaican squash?

Abie: I think it's a squash that comes from Jamaica…

Policeman: Now, if you don't mind, we must take this man into custody.

Cure: Now come on, officer, let's be reasonable. We've only got fifteen minutes left in the show. Why not just let us finish the show and then you can do whatever you want to Tuthrie. *(TUTHRIE yelps at this.)*

Policeman: Well, all right. My wife will be downright furious that I went to the theater without her, but I guess I can wait outside. Men!

(The POLICEMEN march back out the aisles.)

66

Cure: As I was saying…I truly apologize for all the inconvenience that I have caused.

(SEDIEFGE, still enraged with CURE, storms up to CURE. Before SEDIEFGE can open his mouth, CURE pulls a diamond ring out of his pocket and, deliberately waving it in SEDIEFGE'S face, places it on ELEMENOPE'S finger.)

Sediefge: *(Frustrated with his weakness, sings.)*
Diamonds!
Curse how I love my diamonds!
Curse how I love my worldly objects
With optical attraction!

Curse how they sparkle,
Curse how they twinkle!
Curse how I love my diamonds!
Curse how I love my jewels!
(Speaks.) That's it! The wedding's off, everyone go home. Get out of here, go!

(As the GUESTS leave, SEDIEFGE sheepishly crosses to XYZE and they walk home. CURE approaches STU, who has collapsed on the pedestal.)

Cure: Stu, I'm—

Stu: *(Lashing out.)* Get away from me! You say you're my friend, but you stole my bride behind my back and tried to have me killed!

Cure: You didn't have to be killed. The deal was that you could be wounded badly enough that you'd pass out and assume that Elemenope and I had been kidnapped while you were left for dead.

Stu: Go!!!

Cure: You're upset, and you have every right to be. I'll just leave you alone here until you get—

Stu: Go, go, go, go, GO!!!

(CURE crosses to ELEMENOPE and they exit, arm in arm.)

Elemenope: Ooh, can we go on holiday now, love?

Cure: *(Sighing.)* Yes, dear.

Stu: *(Sings.)*
> How can I go on?
> Now that all is gone?
> How can I go on
> When ev'rything's gone wrong?
> I'd found my love,
> My dove from above.
> But she left me.
> So much for loyalty.
>
> How can I go on
> Without my dear swan?
> How can I go on
> After all I've undergone?
>
> I had a best friend
> Always by my side.
> He stole my bride.

68

So much for "friends to the end."

I could end it right now.
But I don't think it's worth it.
I guess I know somehow
I'll climb out of this pit.

I know I will go on,
I'll face the new day!
When ev'rything's gone wrong
I <u>will</u> find my way!
My life will go on!

Stu: *(Rising.)* After all, it can't possibly get any worse than this...can it? *(The STATUE looks down at him and speaks.)*

Statue: That's the spirit, chap. Always hold your head up high, that's what I've always said.
> *(Sings, stepping down from the pedestal.)*
> When you walk through a storm,
> Keep your raincoat on
> Or you may catch a cold.
> If you keep yourself warm
> All your woe will be gone
> And you still can smell marigolds.
>
> So, keep your head up high
> And stick your nose in the sky
> Whenever you feel like sitting on a spike!
> Yes, keep your head up high
> And humm a lullaby.
> So cheer up tike and take a hike!

(STU looks up at the STATUE, unbelievingly. The STATUE has returned to its original, unmoving position, holding its head up high.)

Mysterious Off-Stage Voice: He's right, you know. There's no sense dwelling on the past. It's not as if a girl like her could fall in love with a low-life commoner, such as yourself.

Stu: *(insulted)* Hey!

(ABIE sympathetically approaches STU.)

Abie: Stu? Are you alright?

Stu: *(Still staring at the STATUE.)* You mean besides the fact that I just got left at the altar and I'm hallucinating about talking, singing and dancing statues and hearing mysterious off-stage voices?

Abie: Don't pay any attention to him. He's not even omniscient and pretty darn crabby.

M.O.S.V.: Go to Hell.

Abie: *(music under)* Stu, there's something I've wanted to tell you for, well, for a very long time. And it's time I just come out and say it.
>   *(sings)*
>   I just want to say,
>   I thought you should know,
>   You light up my day
>   With your joyful glow.
>
>   Through good and bad,

Through sickness and health,
Whenever you're sad,
I'll be there for you.

I'll be there for you
Whenever you're blue.
I promise you this,
With one joyful kiss.

I'll be there for you
Through good and bad.
Whenever you're sad,
I'll be there for you.

We may grow apart,
For such things happen.
Whatever fate brings,
You'll stay in my heart.

As years come and go,
Our lives will change, too.
But through rain and snow,
I'll be there for you.

Stu and Abie: *(sing)*
I'll be there for you.

I'll be there for you,
Whenever you're blue.
I promise you this,
With one joyful kiss.

I'll be there for you,
Through good and bad.
Whenever you're sad,
I'll be there for you.

I'll be there for you.

Abie: *(Speaks.)* Stu, the road of life is full of unexpected forks and knives in the road. Sometimes you'll run over one and get a flat tire. But no matter what happens, the show must go on.

(The COMPANY begins to enter and the lights suddenly go dead. Awkward silence.)

Various Members of the Orchestra: Umm...we can't read our music...

Stage Manager: *(From backstage.)* Shi... *(Yelling at someone.)* Get the backup generator running!!!

Conductor: *(To the COMPANY.)* Umm...wanna do it *a capella*?

Company: *(Variously.)* Umm...sure...

Conductor: *(To OBOE player.)* Oboe, can you play us a G, please?

(The OBOE player plays a G and the show goes on.)

Conductor:
> One, two, three, four!

Company: *(Sings.)*
> Here in the theater,
> An'thing can go wrong.
> It doesn't matter,
> The show must go on!

Stabbings or muggings,
Jabbings or thuggings,
Still doesn't matter,
The show must go on!

(Lights suddenly return, with the orchestra.)

Sandbags may fall,
Set parts may break,
Cupid may call
During an earthquake.

Actors may miss cues
Taking a quick snooze.
Whatever goes wrong,
The show must go on!

Conductor: *(Sings.)*
Cell phones may go off.

Company:
Actors may cough.
(They cough.)
Even for a moron,
The show must bore on!

Elemenope: *(hugging CURE over-enthusiastically.)*
I got my Cure.

Cure: *(not so enthusiastically.)*
I got…her.

Tuthrie: *(winking at the DANCER GIRLS as he's hand-cuffed by the POLICEMEN.)*
I got my lasses!

73

High Jack: *(holding his stomach painfully in one hand and a sign reading "I'm O.K. Mom!" in the other hand. His head is now bandaged, as well.)*
> I got five stitches.

Stu & Abie: *(Sing.)*
> We'll wait and see
> If it will work out.

Sediefge: *(Sings.)*
> I'll kick and shout—

Xyze: *(Sings.)*
> While rubbing his ruby.

(The COMPANY forms a line and they begin to can-can. Gradually, everything—the orchestra and the dancing—falls apart until it is all just one big chaotic mass of confusion.)

Company: *(Sings.)*
> Things happen, things change.
> Though it may seem strange,
> Whatever goes wrong,
> The show must go on!
>
> Stabbings or muggings,
> Jabbings or thuggings,
> Still doesn't matter,
> The show must go on!

(The chaos is suddenly brought back into order.)

The show must go on!⁵

(The STATUE steps forward cutting the COMPANY in half.)

Statue: *(Music under.)* So hold your head up high!

Finis

---

⁵ Same as before. By this point, the audience will hopefully be trained. If they are, congratulate them. If not, go with the flow.